Praise for Soul Power to Your Message (the first version)

This book rocked! **Soul Power to Your Message** is a must-read book for any entrepreneur looking to make a big impact. At first blush, it might seem like another presentation guide—but this is SO much more. Michelle is truly gifted at helping people get right to the very core of their most powerful and authentic message. She asks just the right questions to cut through the noise and help clarify that one singular message that only you can own. And she encourages you every step of the way. I am very clear on my message, but I have to say that going through Michelle's book cover-to-cover, I unearthed new insights and am much more focused about how I spread my message. Honestly—I wish I had this book when I was first starting out in business. It would have saved me a LOT of confusion and struggle around my right message and story. I'll be suggesting all my clients pick up a copy of this book—it's THAT good.

Stephanie Pollock, **Business Activator + Leadership Coach, StephaniePollock.com**

Before reading **"Soul Power to Your Message"** I had a few vague pointers and bits of knowledge about public speaking. I had a message but the only place it lived was my heart and my head as well as jumbled in a few blog posts. Michelle has done an amazing job of not only allowing me to get crystal clear about my message, but organizing it in such a way that I can use it for speaking, blogging, writing my book and attracting more of my ideal clients. (Not to mention leaving my legacy!)

My favorite part was the Expression Élan. It allowed me to become more comfortable in my own natural authenticity while speaking my own message. What a relief! Before, I had tried to force myself to be professional and serious, which my audience would see right through. Not fun.

Thank you, Michelle, for writing this book! Everyone that is passionate about their message and wants to get it out into the world must have this book! Seriously. It's so concise, clear, and easy to follow. I just love it.

Andrea Owen, **Coach, yourkickasslife.com**

Just finished Soul Power to Your Message! LOVED IT! I appreciate your sharing and openness and the exercises were really helpful, which is saying something since I have read a lot of these 'get to your message' books! I appreciate how you walked me through it bit by bit so it didn't seem so overwhelming to come up with my message–hand holding that didn't feel like hand holding. I loved your message at the end, it really felt like you were rooting for me and cheering me on!

Nancy Jane Smith, **Live Happier Counseling, www.nancyjanesmith.com**

SOUL POWER

TO YOUR

MESSAGE

THE PRESENTATION SKILLS GUIDE
TO MAKING A REAL IMPACT
WITH YOUR LIFE-CHANGING MESSAGE

MICHELLE BARRY FRANCO

Soul Power to Your Message

The Presentation Skills Guide to Making a Real Impact with Your Life-Changing Message

Copyright © 2012 by 3 SASS Lane LLC

3 SASS Lane LLC
PO Box 4273
Charlottesville, VA 22905

Ordering Information:
Quantity sales. Special discounts are available on quantity purchases by corporations, associations, and others. For details, contact the author at: **hello@michellebarryfranco. com**.

Printed in the United States of America

Manuscript Edit by James Franco (the best James Franco ever)
Interior design by Adina Cucicov, Flamingo Designs
Cover design by Russ McIntosh, Studio Absolute

Content examples and expertise made possible by the hundreds of clients, students and training and workshop participants Michelle has had the honor to teach and coach.

ISBN-13: 978-0615698021 (3 SASS Lane, LLC)
ISBN-10: 0615698026

www.michellebarryfranco.com

Dedication

This book is dedicated to every soul-inspired messenger committed
to changing real lives with your message. You make the world a
better place every day with your courage and passion.
Thank you from the center of my soul.

And to my Gramma, who taught me by example that bold
self-expression is the only way to live a long, hearty life.
Thank you for all your glorious stories, Gramma. I love you.

TABLE OF CONTENTS

A whole golden field of additional resources, training videos,
downloadable worksheets and other surprises await you at
http://www.michellebarryfranco.com/sptym.

You will need the password: **BrightCourage** to access that page. Enjoy!

INTRODUCTION

Why I Share My Message... And Why I think You Should, Too.

I'm absolutely certain that I was supposed to be a 5-foot, 9-inch tall famous country western singer. I know this because I wear a size 9½ shoe and I have the passion and volume in my voice to match (or beat) any famous country western vocalist you can name. It has always perplexed me that I stopped growing at 5 feet, 2 inches tall (why would I possibly need this size feet at this height?!) and cannot for the life of me match harmony with a living soul.

Maybe this is why authentic, powerful voice is so important to me (the part about my big, harmony-less voice, not my height.) Maybe it's because I was taught to quiet my big voice so much as a kid. In fact, if you even say, "shhhh" in my general direction, the hairs stand up on the back of my neck as a reaction to all those years of shushing.

My Message (with a capital M) became clear to me in a less dramatic way than it has for others. I didn't lose 200 pounds and find myself called to teach others how to do the same. I didn't have a heart attack, waking me up to the stress in my life. Sometimes these wake up calls are a direct line to one's calling and message.

That's not how it went for me. For me, it's been a slow revelation. An alchemy of experiences from birth with the biology I was given. I get it now that this is going to keep on keepin' on, this revelation of my Message. But I am pretty certain that this is the right track, that it will always be about *authentic powerful voice* for me.

Exploring The *Big Why*

It's true I was quieted a lot as a kid (that big voice coupled with a house full of six kids.) I lived in some scary circumstances for sections of my childhood—situations that teach a child to be quiet and careful. I also had periods of normalcy and safety. I knew I was loved. I have lived with varying degrees of anxiety, sometimes debilitating and destructive (including one terrifying three-day, bedridden panic attack) all of my life.

Living with such anxiety, I have learned that speaking my truth—sharing my voice—decreases the discomfort. If I find appropriate venues for channeling all of this extra energy I carry in my body and soul, my life is easier. I feel more centered, expressed. **And when I focus in on making lives better from my speaking, I am immensely satisfied and happy**. It is when I let all of my energy, ideas, desires and passion lay idle in me—voiceless—that the anxiety can wreak havoc on my life (and those around me.)

Possibly all of this in itself explains why I feel so compelled to convince others that their voice matters—that there is a place on the stage (or the front of the room) for their message. I don't believe that you have to live with anxiety in order to be a speaker or workshop facilitator. While it can be a reliable source of energy for the stage, it can also be a detriment if it isn't channeled well. It just happens to be one of the important side benefits for my attraction to public speaking, the way speaking works with my extra energy.

Mostly, I speak because I want to change things. I want life to be better for others. I want to give voice where silence, fear, shame or injustice prevails.

I've been attracted to public speaking as a method of changing the world since high school when I traveled classrooms with an entourage of other MADD message-carriers convincing my classmates not to drink and drive. In college, I traded in images of horrific car crashes for bananas and a book of the many flavors and textures of condoms on the market, showing fellow students how to protect themselves from HIV. I have continued to do my part to clean up some of the messiest and meatiest aspects of the human condition through volunteer work since, always using speaking as my primary method of making a difference.

I speak because I believe that authentic, powerful self-expression is the path to peace and freedom.

Let me repeat that because this is the essence of my own Big Why:

I speak because I believe that authentic, powerful, conscious self-expression is the path to peace and freedom.

And by this I mean personal peace and freedom—and *world peace and freedom.*

And if a message lives in your heart, then finding the courage to step up to the stage and taking the time to craft a compelling message is the way to that world-changing kind of self-expression.

> I speak because there is so much power to make a meaningful difference from the front of a room.

This is why, if you have a life-changing message to share, I am absolutely certain that you should stand up in front of as many audiences as possible and speak, too.

HOW TO USE THIS BOOK

This book was written workshop style. My great hope is that you will use it as a guide—*a working companion*—as you create your beautiful, life-changing speech, workshop or retreat. I organized the book in the simplest way possible to take you through this entire process.

You will find many worksheets, checklists and exploratory exercises here. I understand the desire to skim those exercises and move on through the book. I have done that plenty of times myself. In fact, I fully support you digging into this book whatever way works for you. May I suggest that, when you are ready to sit down and really craft your presentation, you come back here and actually work through this process? *I promise, things will be so much easier this way.*

Here is how the book is structured:

Section 1: The Motivation & Inspiration To Share Your Message

This portion of the book is about *Why*. Why share your message? What difference will it make for you and for others? I talk about the difference that braving the speaking world has made in my own life and business and in the lives of other messengers. In this section you'll hear fabulous stories and insights from interviews I conducted with a few of the most beloved messengers of our current times.

Section 2: Crafting & Delivering Your Life-Changing Message

This section of the book is all about *How*. How to distill your life experience and expertise into that life-changing message you have to share. How to share that gorgeous message in a way that magnetizes clients and collaborators. How to deliver your presentation with authenticity and power. How to organize your content. How to tell a great story. This is the meaty part that will hand-hold you through creating your own life-changing presentation. I promise, you will find approaches and guidance here that you won't find in any other presentation guide on the market today. This one is written for *you* and your soulful way of living and working.

Section 3: The Afterward (& More)

This section is about *Whew!* And *YES!* And *What's Next?*

It's also where you will go again and again to get worksheets, checklists and many other things to make your next presentation even more powerful and extraordinary (because we learn something new every time we speak.) Here we talk about the roller coaster that is common after we brave the stage or workshop room. We pull apart different mediums of speaking and weave in the best ways to handle specific venues, like teleclasses, video presentations and speaking for non-profits.

The afterward is really a during, too. But isn't life such a circular path forward anyway? (*I know.*)

Throughout the book you will see reminders about the online resource page I created for you at **www.michellebarryfranco.com/sptym**. **The password is BrightCourage** (capitals required.) I will update that page periodically so that it remains a pleasant surprise for you when you visit looking for new resources.

THE MOTIVATION & INSPIRATION TO SHARE YOUR MESSAGE

CREATING A SUSTAINABLE BUSINESS

And now that we've properly recognized the beauty and goodness of making the world a better place with our message, let me also state: **a substantial number of my clients come directly from speaking**. I realize this may sound silly now, but I truly had no idea what a powerful impact speaking would have on both my client list and business growth—and on the opportunity to speak more often. It's a fabulous cycle, really.

An Unexpected Turn Of Business Events

As I ventured into business for myself, it was a natural fit for me to get on stage to share my knowledge and expertise. Having taught public speaking at the college level for eight years, and spending much of my high school and college volunteer time in speaking related positions, I knew that being at the front of a room had enormous potential for inspiring change and connection. At the time, I was not thinking of the stage as a place from which to build my "platform" as an expert. It was more about getting the word out and providing a "sample" of my knowledge and personality while also providing real value to people in my various networking and community groups. I was genuinely surprised when people started handing me their business cards from the conference room tables, telling me to call them, before I even made my way back to my seat after speaking.

Not only will your efforts in bringing your life-changing message to the stage bring you the glorious satisfaction of helping others—it will also bring you the lovely benefit of financial growth. **If you craft a message that moves people, you'll have them moving squarely in the direction of your client list.** Talk about a big giant win for everyone!

> If you craft a message that moves people, you'll have them moving squarely in the direction of your client list.

A bit later in this book, you will read stories about some very successful speakers, who are also doing beautiful, life-changing work in our world. Take my story and these examples to heart and **know that you, too, have exactly what you need to go make this world a better place with your message right now.**

I know you do your work and share your message because you want to make life better for others. You care deeply about making a difference in the world. Let your impactful speaking help you build and grow your sustainable business so that you can keep doing your important work in the world. We all benefit so greatly from that.

THERE ARE MANY WAYS TO PRESENT YOUR MESSAGE

When I talk about "presenting" your message, I am actually referring to a variety of ways to bring your message to a group of people. In addition, you may be reaching out to quite an array of group types. Here is just a sampling of the venues and groups to whom you may be presenting your message:

- workshops, seminars and retreats that you organize and host
- keynote speeches at big company meetings or industry conferences
- outreach and community building for your beloved not-for-profit cause
- local (or national) politics
- free speaking at networking events to attract one-on-one clients
- online teleclasses and seminars
- videos for YouTube or other training programs to help attract clients and supporters to your cause or business
- plenty more...

There is a good chance that you want to do multiple things on the above list. That's the beauty of taking the time and energy to really craft a compelling presentation and hone your speaking skills—you can do so many impactful, world-changing things with your message from there.

> You can do so many impactful, world-changing things with your finely crafted message.

Taking your message to the stage means more people will hear it. It means you can have a far greater impact in the world. It also means you will very likely grow your business, get funding for your next community project or compel people in your audience to buy your book or other products.

Clear, compelling, heartfelt, authentic speaking magnetizes people to you and your work. This is good because you are here to make lives better with your soul-inspired message.

WHY YOU MUST SHARE
YOUR MESSAGE

The world is waiting for that message you've got. **There are real people walking around with real pain, real struggles, real desire**—and you are holding the answer to their prayers right now, in your beautiful mind and heart. *In your message.*

This is why you must share your message as big and bold—as far and wide as possible. You worked hard to learn the lessons you learned to get where you are. If you're like most of us with a burning message, you took a long road to finding ease and peace around the issue that you solved for yourself. For many of us, our desire to get out there in such a huge way is fueled by this intense desire to help others find a solution more easily and quickly than we were able to with the resources and knowledge we had.

Maybe you finally, after years of struggle, lost the 100 pounds that was weighing not only on your knees and back but also on your heart and soul. Possibly you found a way out of debilitating anxiety and want to share the immense relief you now experience with others. Perhaps you have discovered that living your life based on passion and freedom is possible—even lucrative—and you want to help others do the same. Maybe you have found that ever-elusive peace with work, personal and family life interplay that you know so many parents ache for in their own lives.

Whether your message is about healthy living, spiritual enlightenment, relationship happiness or another life-changing topic, the world awaits.

Whatever your message, however you arrived at its certainty, there is a whole group of people out there searching for you! This—*This*—is why you must get out there with your message. As soon as possible. Right away. *Urgently*.

Why It Matters that *You* (Very Specifically *You*) Share This Message

You've heard that every story there is has already been told, right? You've probably heard that there are "no new ideas."

Well, whether that's true or not, here's one thing that's brand new and yet to be told... *Your Story*. Your specific way of sharing what you've learned. Your way of supporting others through their own journey to more peaceful living.

Your *you-ness* combined with the learning of a lifetime that you've experienced.

Have you ever been listening to a speaker and, while you've heard this message before (maybe many times), something about *this* time, *this* way of saying it combined with this moment of hearing it, *this special way they are delivering the message*... something in all of that changes everything? Suddenly, you are totally inspired and ready for action. You "get it" in a way that simply hasn't happened before.

That's the magic of authentic powerful delivery—combined with the beautiful openness of a listener (audience member) being ready and waiting for *that message, that way*.

So, see—no one else can deliver your message. Not one person who has ever lived, or will ever live, can share your message, your way, with your story.

This is why we need you out there in the world, solving problems, bringing ease, making life better for those waiting for you.

THE APPROACH YOU WILL FIND
IN THIS PROGRAM WORKS

The information in this program is based on hundreds of talks, coaching sessions, and college classes I've taught over the last thirteen years. I have also interviewed best-selling authors and highly successful speakers—each a heart-centered businessperson themselves. The advice and processes here are tried and true, powerful ways to power up your message and build a meaningful, life-changing business.

I hope you find the process here immediately useful. I built it that way. **I want you to get in front of your next audience as soon as possible—and feel amazing about it.** Please keep an open mind. Some of the exercises in here will surprise you. If you do them wholeheartedly, you will bring elements to your speaking (and communication overall) that will make life so much more fun, as well as enhancing your power on stage.

adj
fully or completely sincere, enthusiastic, energetic hearty; earnest

Thesaurus → sincere → ardent, authentic, candid, committed complete, dedicated, determined, devoted, earnest, emphatic, enduring, enthusiastic, fervent, frank, genuine, heartfelt, hearty, impassioned, passionate, real, serious, steadfast, steady, sure, true, unfaltering, unwavering, warm, zealous

antonyms - disinterested, halfhearted, insincere unenthusiastic

17

Please note that I have created special sections at the end of this book to help you tailor your presentation for particular circumstances. You will find sections on:

- how to offer your workshops to organizations
- a guide for presenting powerfully on video
- tips for crafting a presentation designed to attract donors and volunteers to your cause
- specific things to think about when crafting and delivering a keynote presentation

For more videos, checklists and suggestions for your particular circumstance, visit **www.michellebarryfranco.com/sptym**

My wholehearted mission is to help you get out there and change real lives, as powerfully and authentically as possible, with your beautiful message.

Thank you for doing the work you do. *Your message matters.*

Now, let's begin our process with some inspirational stories, tips and wisdom from others who are doing big work in the world with their messages.

LESSONS FROM SOUL-INSPIRED BEST-SELLING AUTHORS AND SUCCESSFUL SPEAKERS

After twenty years of living and breathing the soul-inspired speaking life, I can tell you a lot about how to craft and deliver a truly life-changing presentation (and I do in the pages ahead). I've done it, I've coached it and I've taught it at every level.

That said, there is so much to learn from other extraordinary messengers in our world. I had the tremendous gift of having conversations with a few of our most beloved speakers and writers today. I want to share with you what I learned from them here. Take from their stories the pieces that serve your great work in the world.

Chris Brogan, Best-Selling Author & Speaker

"I had already known what it was like to not have a voice. I wanted to try having a voice."

Chris Brogan, on the evolution of sharing his message online and then on stages all over the world.

Some people believe that the increasing digital connectivity in our world is a danger to human connection—but not Chris Brogan. In fact, Chris will tell you that his world opened up—relationships blossomed and deepened—when he ventured into the online world in his youth. That digital human connectivity continues to grow and deepen in his business (and I believe he would say personal) life to this day.

Chris Brogan has been one of my greatest business mentors and teachers since I first stepped into the world of online business. He does a brilliant job of sharing shockingly useful business wisdom while touching gently and meaningfully at the heart of human drive and connection. This approach has made him one of the top business bloggers online and a much-loved speaker at conferences and corporate events. He is also a best-selling author of a number of crazy-useful business books, including ***The Impact Equation: Are You Making Things Happen or Just Making Noise?*** and ***Trust Agents: Using the Web to Build Influence, Improve Reputation and Build Trust***, (both co-authored with Julien Smith) among a number of other very popular books.

I was giddy-thrilled when Chris agreed to speak with me on Skype so that I could share his advice and stories with you about how to become a truly powerful, accessible, life-changing speaker.

Let me tell you Chris's story, as he shared it with me in our interview, because I know you will find many nuggets that will serve your message-driven mission. (Please note that everywhere you see others quoted in this story, I am writing from memory and notes from my interview with Chris. It is a true representation of the spirit of the statements, if not the precise language used.)

Our Message Arrives In Nnexpected Ways. Trust The Journey And Keep Showing Up.

Chris ventured into his message as an indirect result of childhood experience. While kids around him were into sports and action figures, Chris wanted to discuss fantasy worlds and comic books. Since he couldn't find common ground with kids in his neighborhood, he began to explore the world online. There, he found rich conversations going on about his favorite topics. He made *real* friends and found a level of support in this digital space that he had trouble finding in his offline life.

This early experience led to a genuine curiosity and interest in how relationships are built online. He became particularly interested in how real human connection was created and sustained online, and especially what it took to become an influencer in the digital space. Chris was very clear that truly meaningful connection could be created across the internet through a number of digital mediums because he had created such important and real connections himself. He also saw it happening all around him for others in his online communities.

In Short, He Found The Digital World To Be Profoundly *Human.*

As the years passed and his interests leaned into the business world, Chris noticed that companies didn't seem to get it about how to connect in a very human way online. So, he decided to write these companies "notes", via a blog he created, about ways these companies could use the online space more effectively. Pretty soon, these companies were calling Chris asking if he would come speak to the organization on one of the blog topics about which he wrote.

This is how Chris Brogan went from off-hours business blogger to paid speaker.

Expect Good Pay For Your Valuable Message.

At this point, Chris was still working at another job while he blogged and spoke occasionally in his "off-hours." He was charging $2,500 per speech.

If you've followed Chris and heard his story a bit, this is where you can insert the one about him going to industry conferences and hiding in his hotel room so he doesn't have to pay for expensive dinners out with friends. He's using mortgage money to fly himself to conferences, hoping something will shift soon so he can leave his day job and still keep a roof over his family's head.

One day, at one of these industry conferences, Chris crosses paths with Guy Kawasaki. In case you don't know who Guy is, he is a popular speaker and author of the excellent, best-selling book, **Enchantment: The Art of Changing Hearts, Minds and Action,** among others. As Guy whips past Chris in the backstage speaker area, he says to Chris, "You're going to get a call for a speaking gig. I gave them your name. Charge them a lot of money."

> In a moment, Chris' speaking value increased by nearly $20,000—all because he courageously valued his expertise.

"What's a lot of money?", Chris calls out to Guy's back. "I charge $2,500."

Turning the hallway corner, Guy calls back, "Charge them $25,000."

Shocking counsel, yes. Yet, rallying serious bravery, when the call came and the conversation got to speaking fees, Chris responded, "My fee is $25,000." After a short negotiation, they agreed on a $22,000 speaking fee for Chris' speech.

In one phone call, Chris' speaking value increased by nearly $20,000—all because he decided to recognize his value. Sure, it didn't hurt that Guy Kawasaki had handed him that kind of endorsement, but it still took Chris' bravery to say that number out loud and sound as though he meant it.

Chris Brogan On Imposter Syndrome, Anxiety And Providing Value

"I'm such a fraud. This is so fake. I have no reason to be here."

It is common for those of us who don't (yet) bring in the fees and high-level speaking gigs that Chris Brogan does to assume that messengers at his level experience little or no anxiety or imposter syndrome.

Not true. **In fact, I've never met a high-level speaker who doesn't experience anxiety and some amount of Imposter Syndrome**—including Chris Brogan. In fact that quote you see above is exactly the way Chris described his own thoughts before presentations in his own speaking career.

When I asked Chris if he ever experiences that pesky, "Who am I to be getting on stage telling these people anything?" feeling (which we call Imposter Syndrome), he replied: "Of course. That's why I make sure to **deliver business value, every single time.**"

Chris spends tons of time preparing, practicing and ensuring that the speech he gives will change things for people in that audience. **This is his way of earning the right to be there—of earning their attention and time.** It decreases his anxiety and quells the Imposter Syndrome. While he mostly takes the speak-from-your-heart/vast knowledge approach, with just some bullet points to guide him (one of his best speeches was one in which he actually forgot his note cards entirely), that extemporaneous, conversational style is backed by hours of preparation and years of study and engagement in real human business.

When I Asked Chris What He Thought Was Most Important For You To Know About Speaking, He Said This:

"Make absolutely certain this speech feels one-to-one. Say their names. Help everyone feel a part of it."

Most of all, this deeply human and connected approach keeps him grounded in the reason he does this work: To remind the world that business is human, *first and at the center.*

And if I might add, based on my jam-packed-valuable conversation with Chris, take this advice with you, too:

> Provide immense value every time you speak. It decreases your anxiety, it increases your value (financially and as an agent of positive change in the world) and it encourages people who can help you make a greater impact (like Guy Kawasaki to Chris Brogan) to refer you to bigger stages with greater impact potential. And finally—never forget your bigger "Why", as Chris continually stays connected to his powerful belief that business is—at its heart and soul—very, very human.

A Note About Being Paid Well For Your Message

It is possible that you are feeling a bit of discomfort at the thought of charging tens of thousands of dollars for one speech. **Having worked with many soul-inspired messengers, I know that many of us struggle with connecting money with our heartfelt passion for the work we do.** For us, it is about making lives better for others. Many of us wish we could leave the money thing off the table and just go on about sharing our life-changing message.

If this is true for you, I want you to know I hear you. I understand this feeling and spent years struggling with it myself. Until eventually, after doing only free speaking gigs for a long time, I realized that the world was not going to demand that I get paid for the valuable work I was doing. **I was hurting my own cause by not inviting *people who needed what I had to say* to invest in the process of learning and growing.** Not only that, I was at the brink of quitting because I couldn't afford to give away my work anymore. I had to support myself! The fact is, **the only way to increase our positive impact on lives and the world is to get out more often and more powerfully, sharing our message.**

To do this, we need that common energy exchange currency we call money. We must eat, provide shelter for ourselves and continue to invest in our personal growth and well-being. We must travel with our message, buy our kids school clothes and have funds to give to our important non-profit groups. **We are no different than the rest of the world in our need for financial stability.** The more stability and ease we experience in our lives, the more mental and physical energy we have for making the world better with our life-changing message.

And remember—there are many ways to share your message, and financial level options. You will likely engage most of them, including:

> The more stability and ease we experience in our lives, the more mental and physical energy we have for making the world better with our life-changing message.

- **free speaking** (for your favorite cause or as a means of sharing a sample of your expertise and inviting new paying clients)
- **shorter or less customized presentations** with smaller price tags for groups you want to work with who do not have a big budget
- **bigger, higher paying presentations and workshops** as well.

In most cases, it is a mix of these speaking events that make up the successful life-changing messenger's speaking calendar. You get to decide what is the right mix for you and your business.

I hope this discussion helps you embrace the opportunity to ask for and receive good pay for sharing your message. Creating a sustainable support system for sharing your message, including bringing in good money from your speaking, is the only way to keep getting out there and changing real lives with your message.

Now, let's move from the business realm into the area of self-care and conscious living via my interview with Jennifer Louden.

Jennifer Louden, Best-Selling Author, Teacher And Retreat Guide

Jennifer Louden is the author of the pioneering bestseller *The Woman's Comfort Book: A Self-Nurturing Guide for Restoring Balance in Your Life* plus five other books for women on nurturing and caring for themselves amidst busy lives. A speaker, workshop facilitator and coach, Jennifer approaches her messenger work with palpable passion and energy.

While Jennifer has done her fair share of keynote speaking, I am most excited for you to hear about her approach to online teaching programs and retreat workshops. I have taken online telecourses facilitated by Jennifer and been a part of her online forums and therefore know how powerfully and authentically she shares her message in these realms. I have heard others rave about her in-person retreats at soulful places like Kripalu Center for Yoga & Health in Massachusetts.

I know that what she has to say about presenting her life-changing message in all of these ways will be immensely useful to you.

The Evolution Of A Life-Changing Message.

> *"It all begins with that spark—that thing that lit you up enough to want to share it. You have to slow down enough to trust it, and write, or speak, or create products from that spark."*
>
> Jennifer Louden, on the inner process of sharing your message.

Let's start with the backstory.

Young and ready to make her mark on Hollywood, twenty-something Jennifer Louden was determined she would be a screenwriter. She spent her days smoking cigarettes in her worn-out, way-too-cool leather jacket, penning storylines onto spiral notebook paper. When she finished writing this screenplay, she was going to sell it big—*really big*.

Then, suddenly, she couldn't write *anything*. Not a word would arrive, no matter how much determination she brought to the page. She kept rewriting the same two pages of the play, thinking that maybe—just maybe—if she got those ones right, that the next would flow in easy rhythm.

Nothing.

Dramatically, she called a friend to share the horrific news: "I'm quitting writing."

Her friend's reply: "Oh, okay."

As Jennifer describes it, this was a moment of death. "I felt like I had died."

Then, inexplicably and in an instant, the title of her first book came to her. The book that would become a bestseller—and be an early leader in the women's emotional self-care movement: ***The Woman's Comfort Book: A Self-Nurturing Guide for Restoring Balance in Your Life.*** (But of course, she didn't know what a leadership story that book would tell quite yet.)

Rebirthing—The Message And The Self

It would be two years before she would actually write and publish that book. She spent those two years researching what would fill the pages—living a real-life experiment in the ways of bringing comfort and ease to a woman's life via her own. She joined goddess circles, went on canoe trips and read many books—all holding the question, "What does it mean to take care of myself?"

The first version of her book proposal read really smart, like a "pretend PhD"—*and got rejected by every publisher*. A couple of publishers loved the concept and the title, though. So, Jennifer went back to the page and started all over. She stepped away from that fancily written first book proposal and stepped back into the message of her soul... **And this is the part she wants you to really get—to really hear and soak up:**

She went back to that "sparked place" from which this whole book idea began and she wrote the next book proposal from there.

Two publishers wanted to buy that book.

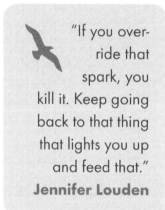

"If you override that spark, you kill it. Keep going back to that thing that lights you up and feed that."
Jennifer Louden

According to Jennifer, **if you listen deeply within yourself, then your message shows itself to you**. It all begins in that "spark"—that thing that lit you up enough to want to share it.

"You have to slow down enough to trust it and write or speak or create products from that spark. When you override it with 'I need to be original' or 'that's already been said' or 'I'm not the expert'... you kill it."

"You want to keep going back to that thing that lights you up and *feed that.*"

On Courage

There is no question that making our message heard above the noise in the world is a big task. Jennifer Louden knew it was going to take courage and real action to get her book out in a meaningful way. She heard that best-selling author and world-stage speaker, Wayne Dyer, had filled the trunk of his car and created his own book tour when he first started out. That sounded like a lovely approach to Jennifer, so she followed suit. She bought a mailing list of "continuing education people" and slapped a bunch of labels on books and proceeded to create her very own book tour. Her book became a best-seller from there, as word of mouth turned to sales and the book publisher began to take notice and then help with marketing.

You can hear details of this process in the audio of our interview at **www. michellebarryfranco.com/sptym**. It's a fabulous story of courage and determination (with a sweet side of young and fearless.)

But the point I want you to take away from this is that you *can* make this thing happen, even if you don't have the support of a big publishing company (*yet, anyway.*) It might mean taking risks that scare you, but that's how most meaningful things happen in our lives, right?

On Self-Doubt

While her early days of self-created book touring were driven by a youthful kind of fearlessness, Jennifer has experienced plenty of uncertainty and self-doubt in her speaking and writing career. In fact, she welcomes self-doubt because she sees it as a possible sign that she is pushing herself to the edge, in a good way:

> *"There are times when self-doubt is an important indicator that there is more work to do. But sometimes it's actually just that little voice trying to keep you safer by trying to keep you small—which is bullshit."*

Yes, most of us experience self-doubt, even when we have deep expertise. Yet, *self-doubt isn't required.* It doesn't tell you anything absolutely. In Jennifer's words:

> *"I taught the same writing retreat for eleven years and I didn't experience any self-doubt. Maybe both are true—there are places and moments where you feel very confident and full. Experience brings trust that you will know how to handle the mistakes you might make."*

When I asked Jennifer Louden to share her best speaking advice for you, the soul-inspired messenger reading Soul Power to Your Message, she wanted you to know this:

There are three things I really work on for presenting. They are:

1. *presence*
2. *stories*
3. *holding the audience (being aware of them.)*

"The worst speaking and teaching is five steps ahead of itself. You aren't actually in your body. You are thinking about what you are going to say. If you stay present to the truth of what you are saying, that will give a transmission—which is what lights people up. The other thing that really teaches people is stories.

Just start looking for the stories that capture your knowledge. Stories unpack it—they go far deeper than anything we can say in summary or abstract."

> *"If you stay present to the truth of what you are saying, that will give a transmission—which is what lights people up."*
> **Jennifer Louden**

If it's about me it's not going to be nearly as effective as if it's about them.

It's never going to come through the way you think it's going to. Trust the way it comes through. If you stay present to it, it will have value for people. You are there for them, develop the courage to be looking at them, to sense them.

Then you can be more responsive to how you need to deliver for them.

Actually, she had so much more to share about how to be more powerful while sharing your message—in a presentation, on a teleclass and in retreats. You simply must go to **www.michellebarryfranco.com/sptym** and listen to it all. It will be worth every second of your time, I promise.

CRAFTING & DELIVERING YOUR LIFE-CHANGING MESSAGE

RADICAL MESSAGE CLARITY

What Is Your Message?

I'm assuming that you have a pretty good overall idea of your message. **You know the struggle you endured or the struggle you walked beside with someone meaningful in your life**, or the vast education you have gathered (probably combined with one of the first two experiences) and you know in your bones the way life feels in the "after" as compared to the "before."

> Your Message is the life-changing gift you have for the world.

This is good. Great, really. It is essential that you know what problem you want to solve and can really feel the benefit of solving it. *And it's not enough.* Because **the solution to that problem is not Your Message.**

Your Message is the life-changing gift you have for the world. It is the essence of what you've learned from hard-core experience, digging deep, trying crazy things, venturing where you never expected you'd go. Your message wraps the solution in a hand-knit blanket of stories, research, examples, and vignettes that resonate with your audience.

> Your Message is more dramatic—and magnetic—than "the solution to a problem."

Your Message sings the solution in beautiful, earth-shaking soprano. The lyrics tell stories of the beloved, the loss, the growth, the revelation. The music draws the shadows and the light into the dance.

See, Your Message is more dramatic—*and magnetic*—than "the solution to a problem."

Your Message Is So Much Bigger Than The Problem Or The Solution.

Let's dig in and reveal your Message (with a *capital M*.). Start by answering these questions.

Revealing Your Message

If you were completely frank about it, **what do you feel you were meant to do with your talents and gifts in this life?**

_____

_____

_____

_____

What struggle have you experienced that you have overcome? Or, what struggle have you helped others overcome that was powerful for you?

_____

_____

_____

_____

What is the problem that caused that struggle in your life or in the life of others around you?

_____

_____

_____

_____

What is the _underlying_ problem that _really_ caused the struggle for you or them?

_____

_____

_____

_____

How is your life different because of that struggle that you experienced or shared with another?

_____

_____

_____

_____

How is your life different because you _solved_ that struggle for yourself or were instrumental in solving it for someone else?

_____

_____

_____

_____

Who else do you know who struggles with this?

_____

_____

_____

_____

Are there groups of people who collectively tend to struggle with this issue? Who are they?

_____

_____

_____

_____

What do you wish you knew "then" that you now know?

_____

_____

_____

_____

If you were absolutely COURAGEOUS about it, **what would you shout from the rooftops** so that others could hear you about this struggle?

_____

_____

_____

_____

What **one secret thing would you whisper in the ear of a person** in the same situation you were in "before?"

_____

_____

_____

_____

If this struggle was not yours but you were instrumental in helping resolve it, **in what way does that same struggle touch your life very personally** and with meaning?

_____

_____

_____

_____

Refining The Core Of Your Message

Now that you've gotten the problem and the solution down on paper in grand detail, read it over. What do you see there? **If you had to put it into one sentence, what would that sentence be?**

_____

_____

_____

_____

What if you had only three words? What three words?

_____

_____

_____

_____

Now, write out the core of Your Message here:

_____

_____

_____

_____

(If you'd like some examples, see the next page.)

Core Of Your Message Examples:

- *You can live a life of peace and freedom, void of fear and anxiety*

- *Your calendar is not your life*

- *Healthy eating is indulgent living!*

- *Your message matters!* (she writes, smiling)

- *Entrepreneurship is a sales job*

- *Passion trumps peace*

- *Beauty is in the little things*

Radical Clarity Of The Core Of Your Message

In order for your message to speak powerfully to your audience, it must first be crystal clear to you. I like to use the term **Radical Clarity** because it really zeroes in on the degree to which your message needs to *speak the truth of your knowing.*

A radically clear core of your message has four qualities:

1. It is easy to remember

2. You can say it all in one breath

3. It resonates powerfully with your intended audience (more on audience in the next section.)

4. You are absolutely certain that it is what you want to say (don't worry if it feels like you can say it even better if you spend more time playing with the language. That could be true, too.)

What your radically clear message does not need to do:

- *Say everything* about your message
- Resonate with people outside of your intended audience
- Rhyme or otherwise be cute or catchy (though it can)
- Give away your solution

Now that you've done a good, deep dig on the core of your Message, refined it and then checked it for radical clarity, let's have it here.

The core of my Message is this:

_____

_____

_____

_____

(Don't worry if it's not perfect. You can shift language as you work on your whole presentation.)

Excellent! Nice work. From here on out, keep that core of your message close. Print it out and post it next to your desk. Write it out real pretty-like in your fanciest artistic writing and draw flowers around it—or skull and crossbones, if you prefer. Just honor and celebrate it. THIS is what you are here to say right now.

Now, let's go say *it*!

THE THREE ESSENTIALS OF POWERED UP SPEAKING

As of this writing, if you do a search on Amazon.com for "presentation skills" you will get 14,172 results. Luckily, you don't have to dig into that crazy stack of books because, really, **these three elements are what matter most in your speaking**:

1. It's all about them
2. Great content, clear structure
3. Authentic powerful delivery

If you simply apply these three strategies to the core of your Message, you will craft a message that makes a meaningful impact. You can move the room, change lives, inspire dozens—even *hundreds or thousands*—of people to take new and better action. You will also, not so incidentally, *magnetize many of those audience members to you, attracting clients and high-quality collaborators in surprisingly high numbers.*

To enjoy all of that goodness, you've got to do a really thorough job of this first essential. It is the foundation upon which the rest of your presentation sits—and it changes with every single presentation. **Be absolutely certain that you give special attention to this essential before every new audience opportunity.**

This first essential is: recognize that **it's all about them.**

IT'S ALL ABOUT THEM

Imagine you have a room full of avocado growers. The Avocado Growers Association has called you in to do a 45-minute presentation at their quarterly gathering. Your expertise is in nature-based cosmetics. The core of your Message is "beauty is natural."

What are some of the topics you might craft a presentation on for this group?

At first glance, you might think a cosmetics expert is a strange choice for this association. And yet, take a moment to think this over... what do avocados and natural cosmetics have in common? Where might these two world overlap?

Any ideas come to you now?

Let me offer a few possible speech topics in light of this line of questioning:

- **Avocado Beauty & the Beast**. A talk on the ways avocado far surpasses synthetic beauty ingredients.
- **Avocado—The New Beauty Regimen**. Ways that people are using avocado in their food and skin care to enhance their beauty.
- **How to grow and promote avocados so that the multi-million-dollar beauty industry stands in line to purchase from you.**

Those are just a few ideas for topics that cross-over between your expertise and the interests of your audience. Now, they may or may not be the right topics for this particular group of avocado growers. To know that, you've got to ask yourself (and possibly some audience insiders) a slew of questions.

You want the majority of the room riveted by your content, your delivery and your clear regard for their concerns and interests. **Which is why you want to speak on a topic that fits that sweet spot between your expertise (natural cosmetics, in this case) and their interests (avocados.)**

Here are some questions to ask yourself as you begin to explore the specific topic you will infuse with your Message.

Audience Analysis Questions

Why is this group gathering today? (for real—not just because it's their group meeting. What do they want from this gathering overall?)

_____

_____

_____

_____

Why did they invite me to speak?

_____

_____

_____

_____

What do they like to do on weekends? Hobbies? Outside interests?

_____

_____

_____

_____

Is the audience mostly male, female or evenly mixed? How might this matter?

_____

_____

_____

_____

What commonalities do we share, me and my topic and them and their interests?

_____

_____

_____

_____

What is keeping them up at night? How can I solve that problem for them?

_____

_____

_____

_____

How will their life be better because I spoke with them today?

_____

_____

_____

_____

How can I delight this particular audience in my talk?

_____

_____

_____

_____

The answers to all of these questions will change the content of your presentation quite dramatically, even while your core message stays the same.

Let me give you a different example to illustrate what I mean.

You are still an expert in nature-based cosmetics. **Only this time, you have been invited to speak at a women's networking group in the fashion district of a major metropolitan area.** How might your actual topic of your talk shift? Would you still talk so much about avocados (especially if there are even better natural beauty ingredients on the market)?

Go back to that list of questions above and answer them about this group of women entrepreneurs in this major metropolitan area.

How are your answers different this time? Make some notes:

_____

_____

_____

_____

Now, think about what you might title *this* talk, considering your quite different answers to that list of questions.

Maybe your talk title would be:

- **Your Make Up is Making You Ugly**
- **Death by Make Up**
- **The Business of Beauty (and it's toxic impact on YOU)**

In this presentation, you share research on how the mainstream beauty lines are using known carcinogens in their cosmetics. You show pictures of the mutations that occur in skin cells as a result of these toxic mixes. You also share the solution that eases their fears—the beautiful, round, plump cells of the skin of someone using nature-based cosmetics. You show the restorative effect of starting right now with the more natural alternatives.

You can see from these two examples how important it is that you build a custom presentation for every audience, even while your core message stays the same. If you don't spend the time and energy on this step first, you may never even get their attention to start—much less make a life-changing impact.

In contrast, if you do spend a good deal of time and energy on this audience analysis section, you will enjoy watching your audience nod their heads, smile in recognition of your stories and laugh out loud (or become teary-eyed emotional) at examples you share that resonate with their experience.

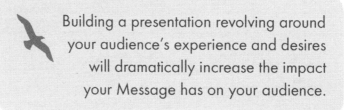

Building a presentation revolving around your audience's experience and desires will dramatically increase the impact your Message has on your audience.

Once you have yourself immersed in the needs and desires of your audience, it is time to start bringing in your vast amount of information. This is the time to dig in and decide what you will include in your presentation and how you will share it in a way they can remember.

GREAT CONTENT, CLEAR STRUCTURE

I bet you have a lot of information about this topic you are going to cover. This is perfect and right. It is your vast experience and expertise in this area that makes you such a great person to be presenting on the topic.

Ask yourself, "What do I know that I could share to help make their lives better?"

And yet, *the best presentations actually leave a lot of information out*. Yes, you read that right. They skip over, remove, and intentionally disregard brilliant ideas, tips, suggestions, stories and examples. This is what you need to do, too, in order to power up the presentation you are crafting. I know that you have been to presentations where the presenter tries to cover everything there is to say on their topic, right? Remember how confused, overwhelmed and eventually tuned-out you were? You are definitely not going to be that person.

Keep it very clear in your mind and heart that *your audience is at the center of this whole thing.* If you try to cover everything you know about the topic—or you tell them too much about the parts that have nothing to do with them—you will lose their attention. This is why a thorough exploration of the needs and wants of your audience members is so important. Only after you do a thorough analysis of their interests, needs and wants do you ask yourself, *"What do I know that I could share to help them make their lives better?"* I call this The Sweet Spot in your presentation; it's a magical place.

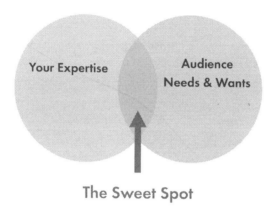

The Sweet Spot

You choose which content to cover in this presentation based on that Sweet Spot.

Let's talk about how to filter through all of your information to get the best content to share in your presentation.

How To Distill Your Information For An Impactful Presentation

As I said earlier, an impactful presentation does not cover everything—*it covers the best information available to meet the needs and desires of your audience.*

Here's how to dig through your vast knowledge and get to the juiciest, most effective content.

1. **Use the usual rules for brainstorming** to get down on paper everything you know about this topic as it relates to this audience to whom you will be presenting. As you know, brainstorming means: set a timer, everything goes, go wild and crazy, no answer is a strange answer—write it *all* down.
   Fun tip: I love to do this process on sticky notes, so I can move the pieces of information around in the next step.

2. **Look for themes** in your information. Make circles around those pieces that seem to go together and draw lines to connect them.
   *If you've used sticky notes, you can just pick up the different notes and make individual piles around a particular theme.

3. When you have your themes gathered, **name those themes**. What set of words would sum up the content of those pieces of information? Write that down. Do you have three solid themes here? **Would this particular audience be *thrilled* to learn this information?** If so, you may have your main points right there.

4. **If you have less than three themes or these themes do not meet the needs and desires of this particular audience, dig deeper** on your topic. Is there anything else you want to add to this brainstorm page? Those one or two themes you have—are they really big? If so, can they be broken into two or more distinct themes? If so, do that.

5. **If you have more than three themes, pick the ones that most powerfully support The Sweet Spot of this topic** (the place where your audience's desires meet your expertise.) Which ones will be most valuable or compelling? Which ones hit the nail on the head?

6. Now, this part is critical—**let go of all of the information that does not fit into your themes.** Even cool data, stories and favorite little nuggets. You can use those another time, in another situation. Right now, you want only the information that meets your audience in The Sweet Spot.

7. Once you have your three crystal clear, convincing or otherwise fabulous main points, get ready to **write those three themes on your outlining worksheet (coming on page 55**.)

I've created some example brainstorms for you to see at **www.michellebarryfranco. com/sptym**. Use those if you need some samples as a guide in your own brainstorming.

Okay, now that you have your information in organized themes, you are ready to start filling out the Presentation Outline.

Guidelines For Filling Out The Presentation Outline

Whether you like to write out your entire speech as you prepare, or you prefer to use "bullet points" to drive your content, **you must organize your ideas clearly** for your audience to follow along with you and remember what you say.

This outline format that follows—which likely looks very familiar to you from high school writing class—**is the clearest, simplest way to organize your ideas in your presentation.** Done carefully, these can be the only notes you need for your presentation.

Some guidelines for filling in this form:

- **Before you write anything on this form, do at least 10 minutes of true brainstorming** so that you are pulling from a large pool of information you could cover on your particular topic (see the previous brainstorming exercise.) The first three main points that come to your mind may not be the best three main points for this presentation. Remember: *It's all about them!* (see page 43.)

- **Write your Attention Grabber *last*.** It should relate to everything you have in your presentation and be the very best way to magnetize their attention in a way that also meets your presentation goals. Your attention grabber is the way you will magnetize their attention, rivet them at the get-go. Because it relates to your whole presentation, you can't choose the best attention grabber until you have fleshed out all of your content.

Clarity over cleverness!

- Your purpose for speaking—your outcome goals for this presentation. **What do you want from your audience?** For example, "I want to convince them to eat more broccoli." Or, "I want them to fill out an organ donor card."

- The benefit to your audience is never "they will know more about [my topic.]" We are all on information overload. **Ask yourself, "How will their life be better because they listened to me today?"** If your topic is the birds of Central Virginia, how will their life be enhanced by hearing your talk? Possibly increased peace from bird-watching? Maybe they will enjoy hiking more because they will be purposeful in their venture? **The benefit you state will be related to the specific audience to whom you are speaking.**

- It is perfectly okay for your transition to sound like, "Now that we've talked about [point one], let's explore [point two.]" Yes, ideally you will add some spice to this formula over time, but remember always: **Clarity over cleverness**.

- **Vary your support points between data, research findings (always cite sources for your research), and stories**. Most audiences—most people, individually, even—need a mix of these types of information to be compelled to action. They need to *care* as well as "get it."

- **Remind them as you close what you want from them**. What, precisely, are you wanting them to do, think, feel? Say it clearly. Give them tools to make it happen (a sign up form, a brochure, a website url on a business card.)

- **Close with *real* impact.** Make your close at least as powerful as your opening, possibly even more so, depending on your goals. Stories, rhetorical questions, or shocking statistics are some ways to close with impact.

With the guidelines above, apply those themes from your brainstorming session and write them in the main point lines on the outline below. Then, take the stories and examples you have for each theme from that same brainstorm and fit them into the support point areas in your outline. These are the stories and examples you will share when you are covering those main points in your presentation.

Be sure to have a variety of support types:

- emotional (stories, images, surprising analogies)
- logical (research findings, data analysis, charts and graphs)
- credibility (citing your own personal experience as an expert, citing reputable references like well-respected academic journals or periodicals, such as Time magazine, National Geographic, or other industry specific publications.

Presentation Outline

Introduction

Attention grabber: (elevator speech, engaging story, participatory exercise with audience)

_____

Purpose/Goal for speaking _____

Benefit to audience for listening _____

Credibility—who are you and why should I listen to you? _____

Thesis: _____

Preview of main points/messages

    1. _____

    2. _____

    3. _____

Transition: _____

Body of Your Presentation (Engaging detail and intrigue abound...)

Main point 1. _____

    Support a (story, example, statistic) _____

    Support b (story, example, statistic) _____

Transition: _____

Main point 1. _____

    Support a (story, example, statistic) _____

    Support b (story, example, statistic) _____

Transition: _____

Main point 1. _____

      Support a (story, example, statistic) _____

      Support b (story, example, statistic) _____

Transition: _____

Conclusion (summarize purpose and main points)

_____

Impactful close (statement, rhetorical question, quote, request)

_____

(As part of this program, you will find a digital version of this outline that you can download to use for every presentation at **www.michellebarryfranco.com/ sptym** reminder: password is in the table of contents of this book.)

As you look over the content of your outline, ask yourself:

      Does this engage me?
      Does it move me to action on this topic?
      Is this content what my heart and soul want to say in service of my message?

If not—if you aren't inspired by your own content or if this doesn't feel like a soul-driven message—then dig deeper. One great way to dig deeper is to mine for stories.

Storytelling

Stories tap our humanity. When told well, they make us care about the issue being discussed—and the resolution of the struggle that is at play. They help us recognize our relationship to the topic. They pull us in and make us *feel*.

Stories pull us in and make us *feel*.

We have more stories available to us than we realize. Spend a few moments answering the questions below to see what I mean.

Mining Your Stories

Here are some questions that help you dig for your best stories.

What is your topic?

_____

_____

What experiences have you had that relate to this topic?

_____

_____

_____

_____

What stories have you heard from others about this topic?

_____

_____

_____

_____

What is your favorite book on this topic? Are there stories in that book that impacted you in relation to this topic?

_____

_____

_____

_____

Have you read any stories about this topic in the newspaper or magazines? If so, where and what was the story?

_____

_____

_____

_____

Where could you go to get more stories on this topic? (search engine, academic databases, ask friends, facebook groups, other social media outlets...)

_____

_____

_____

_____

Just be sure to tell a few great stories in your presentation. Nothing pulls your audience in more powerfully than a story that resonates with them and their desires and needs.

To ensure you tell the story with the most impact possible, here are some questions to help you craft the story that tugs on the hearts and minds of your audience.

The power of a well-told story is big. I bet you know that from experience. Think of a story you heard recently that really hit home for you. Now, what was the message that story was sending? I bet it is easy to recall the message when you recall the story. Stories are really powerful like that, if they are well-told.

You can see an example of my use of storytelling on my blog at www.michellebarryfranco.com/power-of-story-use-your-public-speaking/.

A few of my favorite speaking books are useful guides for storytelling. See the resources section for *Resonate* by Nancy Duarte and *The Power of Story* by Jim Lohr. I also love the way Donald Miller talks about story in his book, *A Million Miles in a Thousand Years*.

> Mixing great stories with credible research and compelling data is the best combo for changing and reinforcing hearts and minds in your audience.

When I talk about stories, people often tell me the stories they have for themselves around how terrible they are at telling stories. It seems we have given storytelling quite an unattainable standard—one that is inappropriate, really. Stories are simple—and yet so powerful. With just a few key storytelling tips, you will be amazed to see how much stories can change the ways you engage and serve your audiences.

Let's tap into those storytelling tips now.

Exploring The Details

First—and most important—Why are you telling this story in your presentation? How will your audience *benefit* from hearing it?

_____

_____

_____

_____

Character—who is the main character of this story you are telling?

_____

_____

_____

_____

Describe your main character in detail (height, age, personality, quirky characteristic...)

_____

_____

_____

_____

What happened to your main character that is directly related to your topic?

_____

_____

_____

_____

How was your main character affected by this happening? What feelings did she or he experience while it was happening or as a direct result?

_____

_____

_____

_____

What surprised your main character in this event?

_____

_____

_____

_____

How did your main character's life change? What did they overcome or learn?

_____

_____

_____

_____

How did *your* life change as a result of hearing or being a part of this story?

_____

_____

_____

_____

How does this story directly and powerfully reiterate or crystallize your main goal of your presentation?

_____

_____

_____

_____

Under which of your three main points does this story fit? Or is it your opening or closing story for your presentation? Is it the very best story you can tell for this purpose?

_____

_____

_____

_____

Use the questions above to help you tell a relevant, interesting story that illustrates a point you are making, makes your audience care, creates connection and helps them relate to you and your message.

Now, if you can couple this riveting storytelling with engaging, dynamic delivery you are going to absolutely captivate your audience. From there, your opportunity to make a real difference in their lives with your message is brilliant.

AUTHENTIC POWERFUL DELIVERY

The first thing I'd like to say to you about delivery is this: ***your best delivery is in your style***. Please don't try to emulate anyone else when you present. Your audience has this special primal reader in their brain (marketing expert and best-selling author, Seth Godin calls this our Lizard Brain) and it sees, hears and feels things that we can't even register all the way. It's a sixth sense. And it tells us when we are seeing authenticity shine (and when we're not).

Your best delivery is in your style.

Let authenticity shine.

I do a lot of work with clients on their authentic style. I am often asked, "What does it mean to be authentic?! I'm being ME. It's just the version of me that is presenting." My response to this is, "Excellent! That's what we want."

The problem is, often the version we are using "on stage" is the "professionalized" (read: boring-ized) version of our style. That's the wrong direction!

It is true that we need to be a different version of ourselves when we are presenting to a group. **On a scale of 1-10, if you are a 7 in energy and effusiveness in regular life, you will want to be a 9 when you present.** It actually needs to be a more exciting version of our natural style—not less exciting. If you are normally a 9, we may need an 11 in energy to be riveted while you speak. We are looking for a bigger, bolder version of you.

> If you are a 7 in energy and effusiveness in regular life, you will want to be a 9 when you present.

So, don't let this authenticity thing make you nervous. Just hold it in your heart and mind and invite the "real you" to step forward in your presentation. Things are about to get really exciting in this domain because I am going to share a tool with you that will help you call forth your authentic self in ways you have never done before. *You ready?*

Name Your Style—Approaching Your *Expression Élan*

There is real power in naming. This is why we have to be so careful about the way we label ourselves and those around us. We know that when we identify too strongly with a label we have been given, it can actually change our behavior and effectiveness.

Most often, we hear about the negative effects of labeling.

But what if we harnessed the power of labeling to our advantage? *What if we deliberately chose labels we could embrace, own and aspire to be more of?!* What if those labels acted like a guiding light in our own authentic, powerful self-expression?

Because they can. I have had the honor of taking many, many clients through this process I created to name their distinct style and I am absolutely floored every time. **When the labels are ones we choose (this is really critical) and they feel true about us yet push the edges of what we know we are capable of, these labels can lead us into the kind of expression we only dreamed of before.**

I have named this deep process *The Expression Élan* process.

While we don't have time or the interactive ability to take you through the whole collaborative process I go through with one-on-one clients here in this book, I can help you get close to your Expression Élan. This process changes things for most people immediately. It brings clarity, confidence and ease because it lays out a way of being that is *truly yours*, yet clearly defined outside of you for your own reference.

Let's dig in.

1. Think back to your last experience of hanging out with good friends—or easy times with family. A time when you felt "yourself." Write down five words you would use to describe your "way of being" in this interaction. If you have trouble with this, ask a close friend to give you a few descriptors but *only use those descriptors if they truly resonate for you.*

_____

_____

_____

_____

2. With your list of five words in hand, go to a thesaurus (try **www.thesaurus. com** or **www.visualthesaurus.com**) and look up each word. Dig deeply into the synonyms and choose an even better word to describe yourself. **Do not ask yourself if others would agree with the words you choose—it does not matter.** You are the only one who has to resonate with these words.

Try this: Take a quick trip to both the traditional style thesaurus online at **www. thesaurus.com** and then the visual thesaurus at **www.visualthesaurus.com** and search a word that comes to you as a descriptor of your style. Any word—just give it a quick search.

Imagine if one of your words was "fun." When you look at the linear list of synonyms, you could choose either absurdity or pleasure, whichever feels more true to you. How might using one or the other of those words as a reference when you create content and choose delivery techniques effect your presentation of your message? Pretty intriguing, isn't it?

Can you see how interesting this can get quickly?

Check out what happens when you take your starting words to the visual thesaurus. Let's use the starter word "professional" as an example:

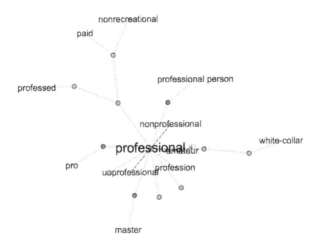

It gets even cooler when you click on one of those words in the word constellation and it takes you to a whole new star! Go check it out. The best part is, this fun process inspires you to go deeper and search for words that resonate even more powerfully for you.

Dig a few layers deep into the thesaurus and you will see some unexpected, yet powerful, words to describe your style. The more unusual your words (as long as they feel fabulous to you!), the more freshness and zing they can bring to your presentation.

Put your revised words here.

_____

_____

_____

3. Once you've explored deeply enough and have a list of descriptors you love, choose three of these descriptors that, together, describe your style in

a way that both delights and empowers you to be more yourself and more fascinating to others. Write those words here:

_____

_____

_____

_____

Now, **use these words as your inspiration to power up your next presentation.**

If you would like to see some sample Expression Élans, go to www.michellebarryfranco. com/DIYEE to download the complimentary extended DIY version of the Expression Élan process I created. This will also help you go even deeper into the process of naming your own Expression Élan.

Weave the qualities that make up your 2-3 word description into your presentation. For example, if you landed on "hip" as one of your descriptors (as one of my fabulous clients did), you will look over your presentation content for more ways to infuse your "hipness" in the presentation. This might mean choosing some popular music to play at opening. It could mean citing some current fashion or cultural trends.

> Your Expression Élan is only for your reference. No one else has to agree—or even know about it.

The important thing to know is that these words are only for you. Let "hip" mean anything you want to you. No one else has to know you are even using it as a guide. And yet, it will most definitely infuse more texture and interestingness (yes, interestingness) into your presentation.

When you consciously infuse your own distinct style—your Expression Élan—in your presentation, I guarantee that you and your presentation will be far more authentic and powerful as a result!

Other Delivery Tips

As you take in and integrate your initial Expression Élan words, let's spend some time focusing on the overall delivery of your presentation. You will want to think of ways to infuse your delivery with that feeling from your initial Expression Élan. It is also time to focus on some delivery tips that we know keep your audience engaged and your presentation lively.

Use your body. Practice gesturing and walking around in the area near you. This will decrease the chances of you rocking, playing with your hair or jingling your keys (yes, that has happened plenty of times. And no, the speaker doesn't notice the sound themselves.)

Just be careful not to pace. If you think you may be moving too much, or in too repetitive of a way, video yourself (see note below regarding watching yourself on video) and see if your movements are distracting.

Listen to yourself when you practice. Let yourself really *feel* the stories, engage with the examples and experience the content. This will help you deliver with natural voice fluctuation, facial gestures and timing. **Listening to yourself when you speak is one of the magic tips to great speaking.** You simply can't manufacture the voice fluctuation, pausing and emphasis that occurs in natural speaking when you are genuinely engaged in your content. If you really "get into" your content, mostly simply by listening with your heart and ears, in the moment, much of the voice stuff will come naturally.

> Listening to yourself when you speak is one of the magic tips to great speaking.

Practice like crazy. Practice when you are in the shower, practice standing at the "front of the room" in your office. Practice in front of your kids or your neighbors. It's uncommon for a person to practice too much. The best speakers—the ones who seem the most natural and at ease and who make the greatest impact when they speak—practice many hours for each presentation (Steve Jobs, one of the best business speakers of our time, was known for spending weeks preparing a presentation.)

Video yourself. If you do this, you must watch it with someone else. **We are our harshest critics. Watch the video with someone you trust who cares about you.** Integrate their feedback with your own reflections. You will learn a lot by watching your video, but only if you are loving, compassionate *and* honest with yourself. Ask your watching partner to give you feedback in the style of a Love Sandwich (no, not that kind of love sandwich. Gasp!)

Here is the Love Sandwich format:

- One thing you enjoyed about the presentation
- One thing you would recommend or suggest for next time
- One more thing you thought went really well
  (See how the kind comments are like the bread of the sandwich?)

Give yourself feedback in this same Love Sandwich style as well.

AMPLIFYING
YOUR MESSAGE

If you really consider your audience and what they care deeply about, you will make a big difference in their lives with your presentation by using the strategies we've talked about so far.

And yet, there's one component of most speeches today that we have left out. Do you know what it is? Have you been wondering about this particular aspect from the first pages of this program?

Amplifying Aids

Presentation Slides

What some people simply call by the brand name, "a PowerPoint presentation" (though more and more options are available all the time for the creation of slides) can be either a useful, important supplement to a great talk–or a terrible distraction.

> Do you really need a slide deck to change lives with your message? Will it truly help?

Let's make sure that you create the former, not the latter, when you use presentation slides.

Imagine this: you walk into the meeting room, find yourself a seat and sit down. As you place your notebook on the table and grab a pen, you orient your eyes to the front of the room. There, on the screen, next to what appears to be your presenter's back, is a presentation slide full of 16 bullet points of information.

How are you feeling about this meeting? Are you hopeful for an engaged, interactive, truly life-changing presentation?

I'm going to guess the answer is, "No."

We've all been in some version of this kind of meeting. The kind of presentation where the presenter erroneously mistakes his or her slides *as the actual presentation*.

In fact, the slides are only a presenter's assistant. The only reason to have a slide is if it enhances and further clarifies information you are sharing.

So, my first question to you is this: Do you really need a slide deck to change lives with your message? Will it truly help? (If the answer is a thoughtful "yes," then I have some great information for you coming up so you can make the most of those slides.)

I don't want to make presentation slides the villain. **It's not the slide programs that are the problem in many presentations, it's the way those slides are created and used.**

In fact, a well-designed slide coupled with great speech content can increase attention, retention and impact substantially. John Medina, in his book, **Brain Rules: 12 Principles for Surviving and Thriving at Work, Home, and School**, talks about the Pictorial Superiority Effect (PSE.) Essentially, researchers have found that we are way more likely to remember concepts that we both hear about and see in image format simultaneously.

The key to the PSEs effectiveness is simplicity— and *meaningful, emotion-inspiring* images. The image must be clear and engaging and relevant to the message. If we see a lot of words coupled with an image, (in the form of text on a slide) our brain tries to make sense of all of those letter characters and we can lose our focus on the learning. In fact, our brain actually sees every letter on a presentation slide as an image in itself. That is a lot of (boring and emotionally flat) imagery for our brains to try to process.

> The best presentation slides have clear, simple images and minimal to no text.

The best presentation slides have clear, simple images and minimal to no text. Let the image on the slide enhance your own speaking to create the most compelling and powerful message.

Less Is More In Slide Design

I know this concept is important because it is one of the most requested topics when I am brought in by a company to facilitate presentations skills training. *Everyone wants everyone else to stop using boring presentation slides!*

Without going into all of the fascinating details of slide design, I'll just leave you with some essentials of great slide design. If you implement these strategies in your next presentation slides, you will delight your audience!

- Less is more
- Use images with minimal text
- If you use text, keep it to six words or less if possible
- Less is more
- Ask yourself, "Does this slide enhance my message or distract from it?"
- Ask yourself, "Will they 'get it' about this slide in 3-5 seconds?" If not, skip it.
- Ask yourself, "Who is this slide for—them or me?" (If it's for you, remove it. Put the information in your notes. Practice more. Don't put it on the screen.)
- Did I say, less is more?

There are some excellent books on the topic of slide design. My absolute favorite, and a classic in the field of public speaking, is _Presentation Zen by Garr Reynolds_. If you don't have this book, please pick it up immediately. You will find it on Amazon. com and at your local bookstore. And while you're at it, get yourself a copy of _Slide:ology_ by Nancy Duarte. With these two resources in your toolbox, you will be in excellent shape for using slides the way our brains (and hearts) most appreciate.

In addition, I highly recommend the blogs of both of those authors. You can find them at **www.presentationzen.com** and **www.blog.duarte.com**. Both blogs are full of great examples and practical guidance for creating truly useful, presentation-enhancing slides.

Don't let your slides distract your audience from connecting with you.

The gist of my message here is: only use a slide when it increases their understanding of a concept or emotional engagement. If a slide decreases your connection with the audience (by distracting them or requiring too much thinking and analysis) or otherwise confuses the flow of information between you and your audience, _it must_ go _immediately_. Be _relentless_ about this.

If you do this one thing when you prepare a presentation—**if you only use slides that truly help them understand while still keeping connection with you** (because they aren't trying to read words or study crazy charts), **you will surprise and delight your audience.** We are sadly accustomed to being completely confused and distracted by slides in presentations. Yours will be a refreshing exception!

✳ **Reminder about slide presentations:** *seriously consider not using one at all.*

When I am asked how many slides are appropriate for a particular length presentation, my answer is usually this... *none.*

Start with zero slides in your plan. Then, **when you notice that you need something visual to enhance your content, think over the many options.** If a slide is the best fit, then move forward with it.

Alternative Amplifying Aids

Challenge yourself to find other ways to expand your audience's experience. Is there a quick exercise you can have them do to help illustrate your point? Is there music you can play or a real object you can bring? Here's a great example of a shocking and powerful "real object" amplifying aid used in a truly great presentation: http://www.ted.com/talks/jill_bolte_taylor_s_powerful_stroke_of_insight.html.

✳ Please go watch that presentation above (the noted amplifying aid arrives within the first few minutes but the entire presentation is stunningly brilliant) before you finalize your next presentation. It will help expand your ideas of ways to amplify your own speech content. (How's that for using mystery to entice action? Aren't you so *curious?*)

It is true that our brains love images—they tap thinking and emotion that text cannot. So, don't toss out all visuals with this warning about presentation slides. Don't even toss out all presentation slides! **Just make sure that the visual aid you are choosing is the most useful one for your purposes.**

Some examples of alternative amplifying aids:

- Activities/exercises with audience
- Music
- Smells
- Tactile experiences
- Actual items (such as the one in Jill Bolte Taylor's Ted talk referenced above!)
- Role playing/skits
- Video
- Their own imagination

 Amplifying aids are an opportunity to truly transform your presentation— for good or bad. Make it the good way!

Well, there you have it. If you've taken your message through this process, you have most certainly crafted a compelling, powerful presentation. You are poised beautifully to change real lives when you stand before your audience.

Now, you just need to deliver this gorgeous masterpiece. *Easy, right?*

SPEAKING OF EASE...

Let's address the five-ton elephant in our living room here—speaking anxiety. Are you nervous about public speaking?

If the answer is yes, then rest easy. You are not alone. In fact, you and I are in the same club. I get nervous before every presentation. The difference is, after hundreds of presentations, I now give that feeling a different description—something along the lines of "anticipatory with a mix of nervous excitement."

> If you are nervous about public speaking, you are not alone.

Almost everyone gets <u>heightened energy</u> when they are going to do a presentation—and many of us experience discomfort from this energy. The interesting thing is, this same energy is what fuels the bigger, bolder moves and voice that you need to be engaging at the front of a room. So, we benefit from it, even if we don't love it.

In the presentation world, we often say that **we never get rid of the butterflies, we simply learn how to put them into formation.** Isn't that a lovely visual? It's also true.

Here are some of my favorite strategies for decreasing speaking anxiety:

The best approach is not to expect to rid yourself of anxiety, but to "manage" the anxiety and channel it into an energetic presentation. Remember, we aren't looking to get rid of the butterflies—only to put them into formation.

Here are some ideas for ways to manage that "anxiety" and use it as productive energy:

- **Breathe:** Big, deep belly breaths—three in a row. Slowly, with intention.

- **Exercise:** Run, bike, take a brisk walk, or dance around your house or room. Burn that energy!

- **Relaxation Imagery:** Imagine yourself at the ocean, quietly contemplating the breaking waves, or on a soft blanket in the center of a warm, gold-colored field of wheat or beautiful flowers.

- **Positive visualization:** Imagine yourself presenting your speech well. Imagine the audience nodding, smiling, and enjoying your presentation. Imagine their applause. Remember this when you are speaking.

- **Say nice things to yourself:** Before, during and after your presentation, your self-talk will have a LOT to do with how you feel about your presentation, and your feelings about public speaking in general. Be honest with yourself—*and be fair and encouraging.*

- **Muscular relaxation:** Tense and relax muscles systematically from your toes to your head. Notice the difference in your body between the tightened (anxiety provoking) state and the relaxed one. See if you can make them relax even more than you think you can!

- **Practice, practice, practice!:** The most effective technique for dealing with public speaking anxiety is preparation and practice. It is infinitely easier to go up and speak when you are certain you have done everything you can to ensure an engaging and impactful presentation.

- **Practice your speech in the same room in which you will deliver the final speech:** Knowing the "view" will help desensitize you to the situation. You will be less surprised by the new experience.

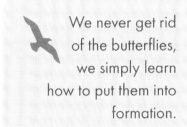

We never get rid of the butterflies, we simply learn how to put them into formation.

- **Take a moment to look at your audience before you begin speaking:** If possible, get acquainted with the new view of your audience while they are still setting up for your speech. Whether this is possible or not, take a moment when you first stand for your presentation to just look at your audience and become acquainted with them visually.

- **Smile!:** When you smile, others smile back at you. You will find this comforting. Smiling also makes you feel good physiologically, which always helps!

- **Use eye contact:** While presenting, speak to individuals in the audience. Stay with one person when you make a point, then move onto someone else for your next statement or point. This will make it feel more like a "conversation". This is engaging to your audience as well.

- **Use your best style of speaking:** It can be very useful to watch and learn from great expert speakers. In the end, however, your best presentation comes from within you and is of your natural style! Don't try to emulate speakers that have styles different than yours. There are many ways to be a great speaker.

Remember, your audience wants you to succeed! If you have prepared specific points, crafted illustrative and engaging examples, spent some time easing your anxiety, and, practiced, practiced, practiced, there is no reason why you can't and won't deliver a great speech!!

Feeling anxious is both normal and useful in the public speaking context. Just remember, the extra energy in your body can actually be used to your advantage, providing you with the oomph you need to deliver an interesting and dynamic presentation.

> Have fun! If you do, it is very likely your audience will, too!

And have fun! If you do, it is very likely your audience will, too!

I recorded an instructional video to guide you through my favorite anxiety-decreasing strategy. You can find that video at **www.michellebarryfranco.com/sptym**. Remember the password is at the end of the table of contents in this book.)

Above All, Treat Your Presentation Like A Conversation.

Great public speaking is as much about listening as it is speaking. Watch their faces for confusion, recognition or other messages. Give an extra example if furrowed brows indicate they need one. Use their eye contact to ground you, teach you and reinforce your brilliant information.

It's a conversation between you and one person, then the next person with whom you share eye contact, then the next... enjoy that part.

Above all, just show up, use belly breaths to ground you, smile at them for a moment before you begin speaking and then *trust*. Trust that all of your preparation and care about this opportunity will come together beautifully. It will.

> Great public speaking is as much about listening as it is speaking.

And remember, if you are nervous, that's okay. That's absolutely normal. In fact, that's how many speakers make their presentations so much better—channeling that energy into extra preparation and practice.

Just don't let that nervousness tell you lies. *You can do this.* You will be fabulous. You've got the message. Now, you've got the tools to power up that message. Go take on the stage, my friend.

Then go celebrate! You are so awesome!

SECTION 3

THE AFTERWARD
(& MORE)

EPILOGUE

Ahhh, yay! You did it! You may not get to flop on the couch yet (you still need to ride out the rest of the event, most likely), but there are some ways you can really make the most of this beautiful work you've done.

Here are some ideas for ways to celebrate the awesome post-presentation bliss:

- **Dance!** Use that extra energy you have from this excitement to shake your booty and celebrate your authentic, powerful self-expression. (I'd love to join you. I love to dance!)

- **Grab three people for a cup of tea** and talk about the other things that are pulling on your heart and mind at this event. Use your energy to dig in deeper to the purpose of your engagement at this gathering.

- **Have that glass of wine you so smartly waited to have** *until after your presentation.* (Do be careful though, sometimes that post-presentation high can make a person a little boisterous with the drink. You are still "on stage" in a way since speakers are in the spotlight even after they leave the stage. Keep your credibility in check by keeping your drink count to one or two.)

- **Go tell another presenter how much you loved their presentation**. Buy their book or program. Ask them engaging questions. Support others who inspire you to keep speaking your message.

- **Have dessert!**

- **Hug someone.** Hug a lot of people!

- Smile at everyone. **Beam!** Enjoy the post-speaking buzz!

Okay, now... I hate to be a party pooper, but I've got to bring up something that has come up too many times not to mention here. I call it **Post Presentation Syndrome (PPS),** and it can be a *mean little guest.*

Post Presentation Syndrome

Possibly you have met PPS's cousin—also nicknamed PPS—Post *Party* Syndrome. This is **that anxious time right after** (sometimes a few hours after or the next morning) **a gathering where you go back over the whole evening in your mind and find all of the places where you might have said something strange**, not listened as well as you should have, made a funny face at someone's story, walked too quickly to the bathroom... whatever myriad of wild fears you gather to freak yourself out about your behavior at the gathering. Does this happen to you?

Yea, it happens to me, too (though way less now that I know how to name it.) And it happens to many of my clients.

I believe that PPS is the result of excess energy left in your body after an exciting event. When we have these intense physiological experiences our brain wants to explain it to us. So, we make up these stories about what we may have done "wrong" to cause this discomfort in our bodies. Those stories are what make up PPS.

Dealing with PPS is simple, if not easy. Sometimes our stories are so convincing that we can't see the PPS for what it is (story is powerful, remember.) And yet, the truth about public speaking, which is the same truth about our behavior at gatherings, is that people are really busy with their own PPS. We are all far harder on ourselves than we are on others.

My favorite thing to say to myself when I begin the PPS cycle is, **"This isn't about me. I am not the center of the universe."** Then I recall for myself the immense preparation, practice, heart and soul I put into my presentation. This calms my mind and eases my soul. It is a letting go. Then I distract myself because I know that PPS is pretty time-sensitive. After a few days (at most), it passes. It's like things that scare you at night—in the morning it's hard to remember what was so scary. Let a few days pass and you will feel that way about your PPS.

> **Calming thought:**
> "This isn't about me. I am not the center of the universe."

This is the perfect time for you to go watch the now famous researcher, speaker, and author, Brené Brown's second TED speech—the one where she talks about her "vulnerability hangover" after her first speech went crazy viral with millions of views (and growing.) It's called "**Listening to Shame.**" It's a wonderful story about post presentation syndrome—and the beauty that can come from having the courage to share your life-changing message even in the face of intense personal fear. Just search Brené Brown and that speech title and you will be able to watch her speech. It's marvelous on so many levels.

And let me give you permission right now to don your jammies for one extra day after your courageous, life-changing work! Languish in it.

Then tomorrow, get back out there and continue bringing your magic to the world!

A Personal Note From One Passion-Driven Messenger To Another:

Okay, my passion-driven friend with a message that *will* change lives—the time has come. You have all of my best tips and ways for powering up the life-changing, soul-inspired message you are meant to share with the world.

I am grateful to you for doing this courageous work. It's not easy to get in front of a room full of people and share your soul's message.

I am also inspired by you. Virtually every person I've ever met shares the fears of public speaking we have discussed. Pushing through these fears in order to make a real impact in the world is brave—it takes strength.

I am also—and really above all—*excited* for you! This ride is awesome. Go get 'em! Change the world, one audience at a time.

I'll be over here doing my work, too. Because we're all part of this mosaic of contribution, making our difference in the way that only we can. It's our job to shine so the whole mosaic shines. We need each other to do the work we were meant to do—share the message we are meant to share. Enjoy the work, my friend. It's awesome stuff. **I'll be watching for you. Keep me posted, please.**

Shine on!

Michelle

Michelle Barry Franco
Archaeologist of Your Soul Crafted Message
(and grateful partner on the path of soul-inspired work)

ACKNOWLEDGEMENTS

I never entirely intend to write a book. Maybe it's the only way I can actually begin, to believe that I am just writing a "short guide" or a simple but highly usable "ebook." In any case, this project went like all of my previous book projects—from small to... well, much bigger.

This means that, without having planned for it, my family has to step up all around me to pick up the slack I suddenly leave. Actually, the truth is, they do that a lot anyway because I do tend to flail about a bit with new projects. Nonetheless, this book took me away from them for days on end on a number of occasions.

I love/hate those writing retreats. I get so much done—and I write things that would simply never occur to me in my usual surroundings. But I miss my babies and my extraordinary, loving husband. And I know they miss me, too, because they hang a lot of gorgeous color-crayon signs on the door when I return home.

Thank you to my unusually flexible and fun family. You light up my world. I do this work, in part, because I want so much for you to feel the same freedom in your lives to shine bright in courageous self-expression. Coupled with love, that kind of self-expression is the essence of human living.

The work of writing the words onto these pages was mine, but the beauty you see before you had nothing to do with me.

If I didn't have my husband Jim Franco's brilliant eyes, vocabulary, and grammar gifts in my life, this book would be a lot harder to read and use. He's a genius and I completely lucked out by finding him.

Adina Cucicov of Flamingo Designs designed the interior of this book, as she has the inside of every book or program I've written prior. She's crazy gifted and a real pleasure, too. Thank you, Adina.

To my astounding luck, Russ McIntosh of Studio Absolute agreed to design the cover of this book on unacceptably last minute notice. The extraordinary outcome is obvious, a testament to Russ' immense talent. Cheryl, I know my "luck" has your name all over it here. Thank you both for being brilliant.

Every day I get on the phone first thing in the morning with Brenna Peyton of One Organized Girl so she can organize my brain and tell me what to do that day. I'm a little afraid I won't be able to survive if she ever stops doing this for me, but for now, I'm simply immensely grateful. This book got completed because she told me to do it a lot of days in a row.

Stephanie Pollock, Andrea Owen, and Nancy Jane Smith all gave me early feedback on the first version of this book. Their enthusiasm made me giddy happy and gave me the oomph I needed to take this project to the full extent of my vision for it. Thank you, brilliant dears. I really, really needed that.

Finally, to my Wisdom Council and my BB group, I am so grateful to you each. You know how sometimes it feels like way too much to handle? You make me feel so much less alone. Thank you from the center of my soul for that.

Oh wait, how can I end without thanking my moms and dad and my siblings. Maybe this book will help you get a grasp on what the hell I do for work, exactly. Probably not, but I don't care. I adore you each and all. You are my anchors in the wide world.

I think I'll carry on with all this, thanks to you all. Especially since things always feel more manageable when the book is done.

APPENDIX

You will find most of the following resources also available as downloadable pdfs plus so much more here at http://www.michellebarryfranco.com/sptym/. You will need the password: BrightCourage to access that page. Enjoy!

Tips On Various Methods & Mediums Of Sharing Your Message

Teleclassses

First, listen to the interview I did with Jennifer Louden at www.michellebarryfranco. com/sptym (password: BrightCourage.) She shares so many fabulous tips on how to get and keep your audience's attention across the phone lines toward the end of that interview.

Here are a few hilights from Jennifer and from my own experience:

- **Start very strong!** Let them know from the beginning that you plan to keep their attention, in spite of the strong urge to multi-task.

- **Request that they step away from their computer and instead grab a pen and paper.** This decreases the chances of falling into mind and soul-sucking computer trance while on the call. No one can compete with that.

- **Tell stories**—riveting stories that have mystery that a person has to pay attention to in order to hear the resolution of that mystery. For example: "When I first started my business I had the most difficult time attracting clients... later, though, I had to turn clients away continually. I'm going to tell you how I did that in a bit... first, let's..." Or maybe something that tugs on their heart strings in a different way... just leave them curious and wanting. Of course, you are going to make it far worth their while so this is completely ethical!

- **Let everyone say "hello" or "goodbye"** or something else all at once, so they (and you) get a feeling of being a part of something bigger than just them in their space, alone.

- If you are using visuals on the computer, **add compelling images that help keep visual attention.**

Video Trainings

I love watching Brendan Burchard's videos, though I know that not everyone loves his highly enthusiastic style (google him if you don't know what I mean.) Whatever your natural style, **be sure to add energy and passion beyond your usual conversational level**. When we are at our computers, our attention gets even more difficult to hold.

Here are a few more tips for sharing your message via video:

- **Keep it to 2-3 minutes per video.** We lose attention after that too often. (If you are doing a "training video" that someone has signed up to receive, you have more time. Just keep it concise as well.)

- **Make sure the lighting makes it easy to see your facial expressions**.

- **Choose a location that has a simple and pleasant background** so it doesn't distract the person watching.

- **Use an external microphone** if possible. Clear sound can really make a difference in a video. If you don't have a camera with an external mic, you can still make a good video, just be sure you are close enough to the camera when filming and you speak clearly and loudly to get the best audio. (There are options for using a recorder and syncing up the sound, but that is too complicated for our purposes here. Keep it simple for now and just get the video created, unless you are a technical expert.)

- Review the tips in the Keynotes section coming up, too.

In-Person Retreats/Workshops

I could write a whole book on creating and facilitating workshops and retreats (and maybe I will.) For now, let's touch on a few things that will have grand influence on the power and impact of your message during the session.

- **Set the mood for the whole retreat from the beginning.** People are curious and vulnerable when arriving to a group event. Make it as clear as possible right away what they can expect.

- **Share the agenda as early in the process as possible.** As stated above, people can be carrying a good deal of uncertainty at workshops and retreats and this kind of care and attention to their needs is so valuable for establishing trust and engagement.

- **Switch things up about every 10 minutes.** Yep—I said every 10 minutes (see the book, *Brain Rules* by John Medina where he explains how he applies this in his popular college classes.) That doesn't mean you have to have an exercise or activity every ten minutes, just that you need to do something new and fresh: tell a story, have them take a small action, ask a question that inspires engagement.

- **Remember that, as the facilitator and host, your job is to provide comfort and ease** to the best of your ability so the good work of your message can be taken in and utilized to the benefit of each person there. You are not responsible for them or how they feel, of course, but you can do a lot to provide an environment most conducive to learning and personal growth.

- **Use color pens, paper, movement, small group work and quiet time** often and freely. **Encourage people to express themselves in as many ways as possible** (drawing, writing, moving, singing—whatever fits your topic.)

Keynotes

Read all of the points above under retreats and workshops and apply them appropriately to your keynote. (Color pens and movement in this case are more likely to be *your* tools than ones they share in—but use them still! And if you can find a way to use a short small group exercise, the crowd will likely appreciate it.)

- Be funny. Unless you are not naturally funny, in which case do not try to be funny. It just doesn't work. **Be yourself, bigger and bolder—be courageous about this**. Make it remarkable.

- Take Chris Brogan's approach and **bring measurable value every single time.** Yes, they want to be entertained and engaged. But you are here to change lives, right? Tell them a story that blows them away, that they can't help but carry with them out the door. One that compels them to take action when they leave. Give them a simple tool to take action, too. Right away.

- **Use your loud voice**. Often keynotes happen over breakfast, lunch or dinner. Recognize the sound and attention struggles that environment will bring.

- **Vary your stories**. Tell stories from your own experience, yes. They are great for credibility and connection. But too many stories about just you (unless your speech is based on your life story) can feel self-absorbed and actually interfere with your credibility. Show us you've seen successes in clients' lives with this knowledge you're sharing, or show your ability to celebrate greatness in colleagues by sharing their shining stories.

- **Don't forget to look at the farthest, deepest corners of the audience**. While you can't really see their faces, they (and the rest of the audience) can feel your interest and care about them with this gesture. Get up on your tippy toes and point your hand (not your finger) in their direction, to show you are talking with them. Do this while really thinking about and talking with them so it doesn't feel like one of those ridiculous politician finger pointing things (why do they do that?!)

Outreach For Cause-Related Speaking

Oh, how many times I wish I could leap up to the podium or front of the room when I see a passionate, heart-centered person trying to gather support (financial, volunteers, donations of any kind) fumble through their presentation! This, more than

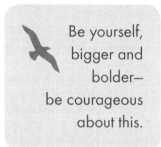

Be yourself, bigger and bolder— be courageous about this.

any other time, is evidence of the fact that *passion and care are not enough to make the profound difference you want to make in the world.*

Here are the top five things I'd like to tell each gorgeous soul who stands up to share the mission of their non-profit organization:

* As you begin to prepare your presentation, **decide what you *really want from the audience***. You will **ask for it clearly at least three times** in your presentation.

* Before you ask for anything from the audience, help them care deeply about the work you are doing. The very best way to do this is to **tell stories that will resonate for them, inspire them to help**—and give them hope through your organization's work. Don't forget the hope!

* **Use any anxiety-reducing strategies that work for you** many times throughout the process and the speech. Don't let nerves overshadow your powerful passion.

* Make the situation real for us. **Bring pictures, video, actual items** (the letter you received from a grateful client or a sample of dirty water that represents the only water available in the area you are helping.) Have us imagine a situation in our minds. Take us on a mental journey.

- **Give us something we can take away**: a volunteer brochure, an envelope for donations. Make sure you have a place we can leave them that day, too, so we can take action immediately if we choose.

- **Commit to a powerful delivery of your message**. Practice, speak loudly, stand tall. This may be a volunteer opportunity for you but it represents huge potential to make a difference in your cause. Take it on for all it's worth!

Some Thoughts On What Kind Of Presentation To Prepare And Offer

My friend and colleague, Don Blohowiak, is the author of multiple business books and was the star of a successful speaking career. Until one day, standing in the bright light of a keynote speaking gig, audience out in the darkness staring expectantly at him, he experienced a life altering realization. *He hated being in the spotlight on stage.*

Don's sudden realization was so powerful that it immediately shut down his keynote speaking business—which was one of the most lucrative revenue streams in his business.

What Don realized was that he felt completely empty up there on stage. He wanted the interaction and engagement he enjoyed in smaller venues and in his client interactions. He did not want to be the "focus" of attention as much as he wanted to be a facilitator of learning and change.

For Don, a keynote speech is drudgery where a workshop is exhilarating fun.

While you may be asked to facilitate a specific kind of presentation—a keynote for a conference or maybe a breakout session instead—sometimes you get to decide. **Remember, this is your soul-inspired message. You are here to change lives with this gift.** What medium or format will thrill you and bring out the very best in your delivery and engagement? Do your best to present in that format every time you speak.

What medium or format will thrill you and bring out the very best in your delivery and engagement? Do you best to present in that format every time you speak.

If the format of the speaking event interferes with your ability to inspire change in people who need your message, then your good work is at risk. **Be sure to ask the event organizer what kind of freedom you have to create the presentation you** know **will absolutely thrill the audience.**

Presentation Prep Quick Checklist

- ☐ What is my main idea?

- ☐ Is it JUST ONE IDEA?

- ☐ Why should they care?

- ☐ Why should they listen to me about this?

- ☐ What do I want them to do as a result of this presentation?

- ☐ Do I have three main points? If not, is it for a really good reason?

- ☐ Do I have a clear introduction that previews my main points?

- ☐ Do I cover each main point in the order I stated in the intro?

- ☐ Do I have a conclusion that includes a review of the main idea or the main points specifically?

- ☐ Do I end with a bang: specific request, powerful story, rhetorical question, something that allows them to take immediate action like a sign up form?

- ☐ Do my amplifying aids truly add to the presentation?

- ☐ Am I using my slides as a way to help the audience remember my points (NOT as my notes for the presentation)?

- ☐ Have I designed the presentation for maximum connection between me and the audience (their focus on me, my focus on them.)

- ☐ Did I leave them with contact information to reach me later with questions?

- ☐ How is the time I spend creating this presentation—and the time the audience spends listening to it—going to make life better for them (and me... and the world)?

- ☐ Is this the shortest presentation I can possibly do really well on this topic?

How To Create An Image-Based Slide In PowerPoint

Once you are clear what your driving message is for your slide, come up with a concept that would best represent the idea. Write down a few key terms to describe the concept. For example: Boring Presentations—"sleeping in meeting", "hazy room", "boring business."

Go to your favorite image source (e.g. istockphoto.com, flickr.com, fotolio.com) **and search your terms.**

If you have no budget for images, you can use Flickr.com or one of the other free image resources. Just be sure you adhere to their copyright rules. Flickr has a fabulous Creative Commons area where you can use images shared by others as long as you give attribution to the photographer. In the "Explore" tab, click "Creative Commons." You will find millions of images that others have offered for your use simply by giving attribution (citing their Flickr name and sometimes a link) with varying levels of additional requirements, such as no modification of the image.

I like to choose the **"Attribution License" option** (click where it says, "see more") because it has the least restriction on how I use the image. When you get into the "Attribution License" area by clicking "see more", you can search those key terms you jotted down earlier.

When you find the image you would like to use, click "actions" then "view all sizes" and choose the size you would like to download. Large is good for a slide project.

Download the image to a folder you will be able to access later.

Now, you have two options for filling your slide with an image: background or picture. If you do not care to link your image to anything (like a url), then right click on your slide and choose "format background." Choose "picture" and then "choose a picture" to browse to the image you saved in a folder on your computer.

If you do want the image to link to something, you will need to insert a picture then create a link. **Go back to your blank PowerPoint slide and, at the top PowerPoint menu, click "Insert" then "picture" then browse to the image you downloaded.** Crop, stretch or otherwise manipulate that picture to fit the screen as you wish.

To insert a link connected to the image, click on the image then create a hyperlink to that image in the same way you add hyperlinks to other objects or text in your slide program. (It varies by program but usually involves some version of clicking "Insert" then "Hyperlink" from the toolbar.)

If you'd like to add text to a full-image slide, click "Insert" then "text box". Select the entire text box and click on a color in the formatting palette that will fill that box. Then type your text into the text box so that the text box and its text will lay over your image.

Voila! You have a visually powerful, "story rich", emotion-inspiring slide!

(see www.presentationzen.com or www.duarte.com.blog for examples of image-based slides.)

Presentation Resources To Power Up Your Message

Speaking Skills/Content

Confessions of a Public Speaker by Scott Berkun

Fun read with many anecdotes from Scott's years as a professional speaker. Plenty of practical advice you can use right away.

Fascinate: Your 7 Triggers to Persuasion and Captivation by Sally Hogshead

A...well, *fascinating* book full of both theory and practical tips on ways to be more captivating and persuasive in your communication.

How We Decide by Jonah Lehrer

An accessible resource for understanding the way our brains work in decision-making. Useful for crafting messages that allow people to take decisive action ASAP from your speaking.

Made to Stick by Chip Heath & Dan Heath

Oh so many good stories in here to illustrate the difference between messages that stick with the listener and those that just pass through consciousness, like the cackling witch swooshing across the moon image on a hokey Halloween show.

Presentation Secrets of Steve Jobs by Carmine Gallo

Since Steve Jobs was an absolute magician on stage, he makes for abundant examples of great speaking techniques that inspire a roomful of people.

Presenting to Win: The art of telling your story by Jerry Weissman

Jerry Weissman has coached many heavy-hitters in venture capital and other parts of the business world and facilitated many big-money deals as a result. This book encapsulates the highly successful process he takes clients through.

Start with Why by Simon Sinek

Simon says (tee hee) that people aren't persuaded by your "what" (product, service, opportunity), they are inspired to take action based on your "why." This book is about how to get to your *real* why then express it in a way that inspires others to join in.

Switch by Chip Heath & Dan Heath

Chip & Dan are brilliant students and teachers of powerful, effective communication. This book is about how to harness the emotional and rational mind to evoke meaningful change in yourself and others.

Transformational Speaking by Gail Larsen

Highly spiritual and heart-centered, Gail's approach to speaking—and especially speech anxiety—is fascinating and useful for those who connect powerfully with soulful messages. An unusual lens into speaking that is worth exploring if businessy type books don't "speak your language."

Amplifying Aids

Presentation Zen by Garr Reynolds

The golden treasure of all presentation slide books! If you take Garr's advice to heart, you will create beautiful and wonderfully effective slides—and they don't require a lot of design skill. His techniques are simple. *You must read this before you do any presenting with slides.*

Presentation Zen Design by Garr Reynolds

The technical follow-up to Presentation Zen for those who want to take their slide creation skills to the next level of precision. A beautiful visual experience, just like Presentation Zen.

Slide:ology: The art and science of creating great presentations by Nancy Duarte

Nancy generously shares her tips and techniques for building highly effective slide decks for powerhouses like Al Gore and Google. Great content tips as well as visual design guidance.

The Back of the Napkin by Dan Roam

The coolness of the advice in this book goes way beyond presentation design. Use drawings to help you think through your content, explore topics, clarify concepts for yourself as well as for your audience. And definitely explore the idea of using hand drawings as Visual Aids in your presentations. The real-time nature of them is quite powerful if used well.

Overall Speaking Strategies

Brain Rules: 12 Principles for Surviving and Thriving at Work, Home and School by John Medina

The cool stuff I learned in this book about the way our brain works has changed my own presentations dramatically. This book teaches you neuroscience in a way that feels like you're indulging in a delicious afternoon tryst with a fabulous novel.

> **There are just too many great resources to list here.
> Visit **www.michellebarryfranco.com/sptym** for the most updated list.
> (Top secret reminder: The password is in the Table of Contents.)

Presentation Outline

Introduction

Attention grabber: (elevator speech, engaging story, participatory exercise with audience)

_____

Purpose/Goal for speaking _____

Benefit to audience for listening _____

Credibility—who are you and why should I listen to you? _____

Thesis: _____

Preview of main points/messages

    1. _____

    2. _____

    3. _____

Transition: _____

Body of Your Presentation (Engaging detail and intrigue abound...)

Main point 1. _____

    Support a (story, example, statistic) _____

    Support b (story, example, statistic) _____

Transition: _____

Main point 1. _____

    Support a (story, example, statistic) _____

    Support b (story, example, statistic) _____

Transition: _____

Main point 1. _____

      Support a (story, example, statistic) _____

      Support b (story, example, statistic) _____

Transition: _____

Conclusion (summarize purpose and main points)

_____

Impactful close (statement, rhetorical question, quote, request)

_____

ABOUT THE AUTHOR

Michelle Barry Franco, M.A., CPC is committed to making it easy and joyful for soul-inspired people with a life-changing message to make a real difference in the lives of those who need them. She has helped hundreds of individuals become more confident and engaging in their speaking and writing. For the last five years, Michelle has focused on helping coaches, therapists, artists and wellness professionals build businesses based on their life-changing message. Michelle also coaches, consults and facilitates trainings for organizations who are committed to authentic, engaging business communication.

She facilitates speaking workshops and trainings and provides speaking and writing coaching across the country in person and through the magic of digital technology at **www.michellebarryfranco.com** and **www.mbfprofessionaldevelopment.com**. Visit her websites for more information on her speaking and other services as well as free gifts and resources to help facilitate your most authentic, powerful communication.

Notes

Notes

Notes

Would you like more support for sharing your life-changing message with the world?

You are warmly and enthusiastically invited to sign up for free trainings and other goodies at www.michellebarryfranco.com.

Let's stay connected!

Made in the USA
Charleston, SC
19 December 2012